THE DRAGON
and the
WILD FANDANGO

by Patty Wolcott
illustrated by Bill Morrison

♦ ADDISON-WESLEY

*"To all children
who are learning to read"*

FIRST READ-BY-MYSELF BOOKS
by PATTY WOLCOTT

Beware of a Very Hungry Fox
The Cake Story
Double-Decker, Double-Decker, Double-Decker Bus
The Dragon and the Wild Fandango
The Forest Fire
I'm Going to New York to Visit the Queen
The Marvelous Mud Washing Machine
My Shadow and I
Pickle Pickle Pickle Juice
Super Sam and the Salad Garden
Tunafish Sandwiches
Where Did That Naughty Little Hamster Go?

Text Copyright © 1980 by Patty Wolcott
Illustrations Copyright © 1980 by Bill Morrison
All Rights Reserved
Addison-Wesley Publishing Company, Inc.
Reading, Massachusetts 01867
Printed in the United States of America
ABCDEFGHIJK-WZ-89876543210

Library of Congress Cataloging in Publication Data

Wolcott, Patty, 1929–
  The dragon and the wild fandango.
  SUMMARY: A dragon joins a group dancing a fandango.
  [1. Dancing—Fiction. 2. Dragons—Fiction]
I. Morrison, Bill, 1935– II. Title.
PZ7.W8185Dr   [E]   79-23515
ISBN 0-201-08733-2

Sprightly

Dance a fandango, a

wild fandango.

Come dance a wild dance, a

wild dance fandango.

Will you come dance, dragon,

dance a fandango?

Come dragon, dance dragon

dance.